D1824008

Opening Gifts

Sherry Gieser

Confirmation

Includes a Parent-Teacher Guide

Our Sunday Visitor Publishing Division
Our Sunday Visitor, Inc.
Huntington, Indiana 46750

Illustrated by Kevin Davidson

Nihil Obstat:
Very Reverend Jay H. Peterson
Vicar General, Diocese of Great Falls-Billings
Imprimatur:
✠ Anthony M. Milone
Bishop of the Diocese of Great Falls-Billings
November 1, 2001

The *Nihil Obstat* and *Imprimatur* are official declarations that
a book or pamphlet is free of doctrinal or moral error. No
implication is contained therein that those who have granted
the *Nihil Obstat* and *Imprimatur* agree with the contents,
opinions, or statements expressed.

Every reasonable effort has been made to determine copyright
holders and to secure permissions as needed. If any copyrighted
materials have been inadvertently used without proper credit
being given in one manner or another, please notify
Our Sunday Visitor in writing so that future editions
may be corrected accordingly.

Copyright © 2002 by Our Sunday Visitor Publishing Division,
Our Sunday Visitor, Inc. All rights reserved.

With the exception of short excerpts for critical review, no part
of this book may be reproduced or transmitted in any form or
by any means, electronic or mechanical, including photocopying,
recording, or by any information storage or retrieval system,
without permission in writing from the publisher:
Write:

Our Sunday Visitor Publishing Division
Our Sunday Visitor, Inc.
200 Noll Plaza
Huntington, IN 46750

ISBN: 1-931709-07-6 (Inventory No. R7)

Cover and interior design by Monica Haneline
Cover and interior art by Kevin Davidson

PRINTED IN THE UNITED STATES OF AMERICA

Celebrations are fun!

Draw a picture or write about a
celebration you remember.

God wants us to c _ _ _ _ _ _ _ _
His love for us. He wants
us to celebrate His
p _ _ _ _ _ _ _ with us.

ABMTPSI

_____

TYOMIMRNA

_____

FNNOOCRIIAMT

_____

Sacraments are a special way
we can celebrate with God.
Can you unscramble the names
of the seven sacraments
of the Church?

HTAICERUS

_____

NNTANIGIO FO ETH KSCI

_____ __ ___ ____

EIRILAONNICOCT

_____

LYOH DORSRE

_____ _____

In the first sacrament, Baptism,
we are delivered from original sin
and w _ _ _ _ _ _ _ into
the family of God.

This sacrament actually has a partner,
the sacrament of Confirmation
(which means "making stronger").

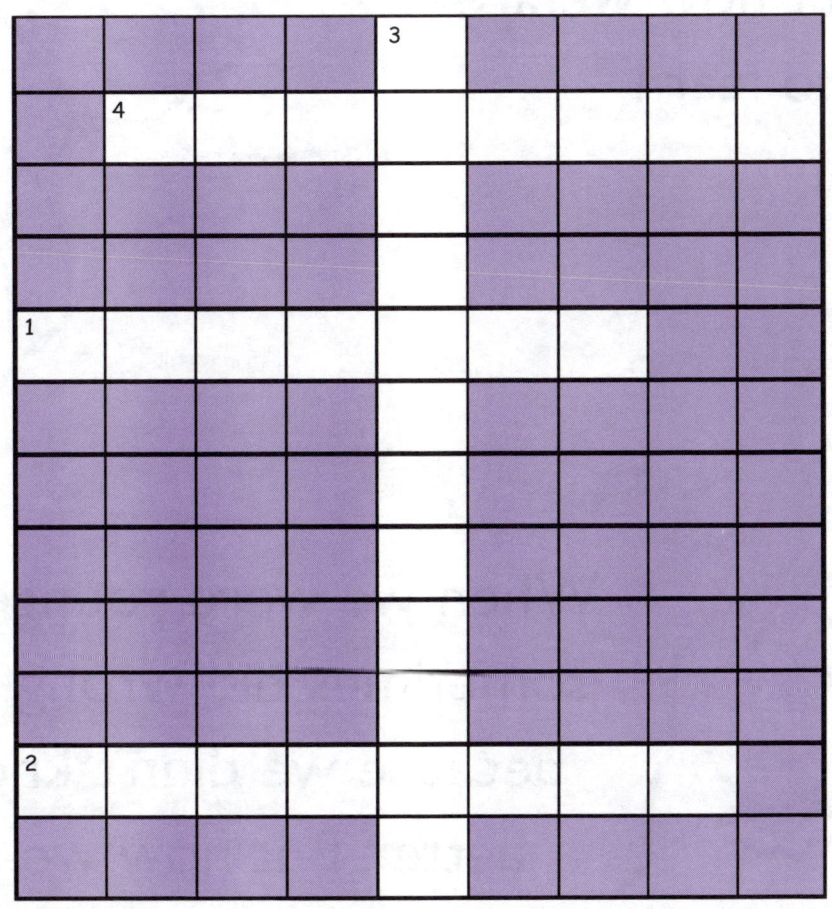

Fill in the crossword puzzle above using the clues in the sentences below.

In the sacrament of (1___), we are (2___) into the Church. The sacrament of (3___) makes us (4___) Christians.

Many people are babies when they are baptized. When we were babies, we could not do things by ourselves. But now we are old enough to learn about Jesus.

When we were younger, we sometimes did wrong things because we didn't know any better. But now we are old enough to learn what is right and what is wrong. We are old enough to make good choices.

Jesus asks us to follow Him and be like Him.

What are some good choices we could make that would make us more like Jesus?

Jesus knows that sometimes it is hard for us to be good. He wants to help us, so He gives us the gift of His Holy Spirit.

Confirmation is the c _ _ _ _ _ _ _ _ _ _ of this gift!

Jesus was also called *Christ*, which means "the anointed one" of God. When Jesus was on earth, He laid His hands upon people and they were blessed.

Sometimes He performed miracles this way. Jesus Christ promised the apostles that He would send His Holy Spirit to be with them always. After Jesus went to heaven, His apostles were filled with the Holy Spirit. They, too, began to do great things. Read the story of Pentecost in the Bible (Acts 2:1-4, 43 and 3:1-10).

When the Holy Spirit came upon the apostles, they were not afraid. When other people wanted to believe in Jesus, the apostles laid their hands upon them and prayed that they also could receive the Holy Spirit. The apostles also anointed them with oil, as a sign that they, too, were becoming "anointed ones," who were called *Christians*. The bishops, the successors of the apostles, continue this ancient tradition to the present day.

When it is your turn to be confirmed, the bishop will lay his hands on you and anoint you with the oil called *holy chrism*. He will ask God to seal you with the gift of the Holy Spirit. What a great present the Holy Spirit is!

WORDFIND

```
C   B   E   L   I   E   V   E   R
H   O   A   Y   L   D   M   S   E
O   T   N   E   S   E   R   P   B
L   L   M   F   G   L   V   K   I
Y   B   K   B   I   S   H   O   P
D   C   R   O   F   R   F   C   Q
S   H   S   G   T   E   M   J   F
P   R   E   C   E   I   V   E   P
I   I   A   T   U   G   X   O   D
R   S   L   C   H   A   N   D   S
I   M   H   J   P   U   O   A   H
T   R   A   D   I   T   I   O   N
```

Find the following words. The words are in all directions — even backward!

BELIEVE	CONFIRMED	BISHOP	PRESENT
RECEIVE	HANDS	OIL	SEAL
GIFT	TRADITION	CHRISM	HOLY SPIRIT

The Holy Spirit brings even more gifts
with Him. Our Church has names
for seven of His gifts.

Gifts of the Holy Spirit

1. **Piety** (or Reverence) — The strength to live the greatest commandment: "Love the Lord your God with your whole heart, your whole soul, and your whole mind."

2. **Fear of the Lord** (or Wonder and Awe in God's Presence) — The recognition that God is our strongest defense against all evil. The beginning of wisdom.

3. **Wisdom** — The ability to see how all things work together as God sees it.

4. **Counsel** (or Right Judgment) — The willingness to turn to God for direction.

5. **Understanding** — Having a heart close to God's so we can know right from wrong.

6. **Knowledge** — The ability to discover the path in life God wants us to follow.

7. **Fortitude** (or Courage) — The ability to face things we are afraid of by knowing that God is our bodyguard.

After you have read and talked about these gifts, make up a situation where a person like you might need to use each one of these gifts.

Piety -
_____
- -
_____
- -
_____

Fear of the Lord - - - - - - - - - - - - - - - - - -
_____
- -
_____
_____
- -

Wisdom -
_____
- -
_____
_____
- -

Counsel

Understanding

Knowledge

Fortitude

God has given us these gifts. But many people never open them, so they never feel the Holy Spirit in themselves. We must choose to open these gifts. But how do you open an invisible gift?

Simply by praying.

Praying to God can open any gift. But if we don't use the gift, it can wither away like a plant without water.

By continuing to pray, and by using our gifts as often as possible, they grow stronger and stronger.

Each time we use our gifts, we grow closer to Jesus. When this happens, it is easier for us to do the good things that Jesus asks us to do. That is when the Holy Spirit bears spiritual fruit through us.

Fruits of the Holy Spirit

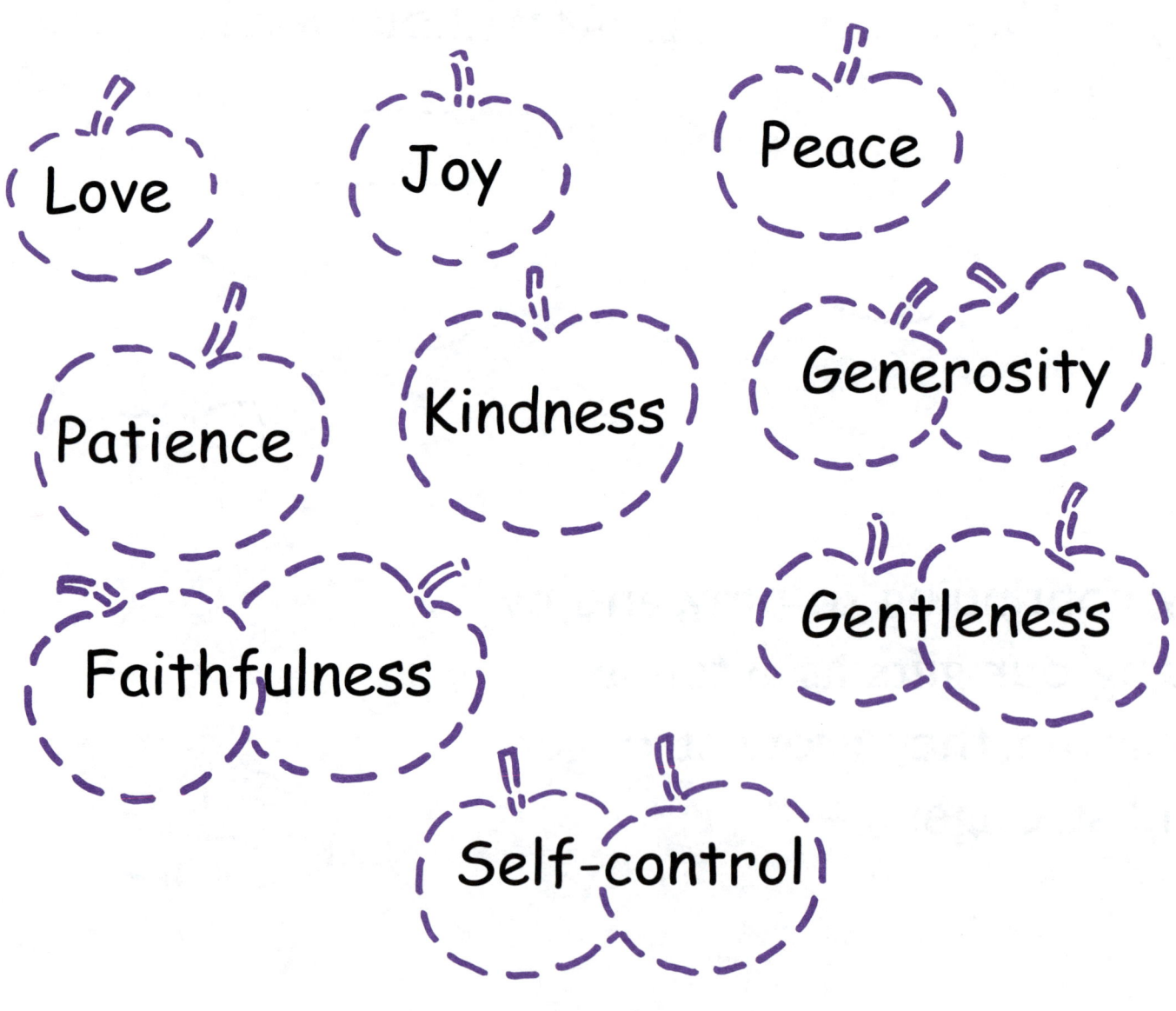

Love

Joy

Peace

Patience

Kindness

Generosity

Faithfulness

Gentleness

Self-control

Write in the fruits of the Holy Spirit.

When we take in and use the seven gifts of the Holy Spirit, we can produce the nine fruits of the Holy Spirit.

When we feel these things, like joy and peace,
we know the Holy Spirit is working in us.

The sacrament of Confirmation is only received once, so we must take care of our gift of the Holy Spirit. Here is an easy prayer you can say:

Come, Holy Spirit, be with me. Amen.

The best prayer we can pray to strengthen our gifts is the big prayer called the *Mass*. To stay strong, we should do this at least once a week. There we can nourish the Holy Spirit in us with the prayers of our friends and family.

We also strengthen the Holy Spirit in us by hearing the Word of God from the Bible.

Best of all, we can feed this holy presence with the very Body and Blood of Jesus in the sacrament of the Eucharist.

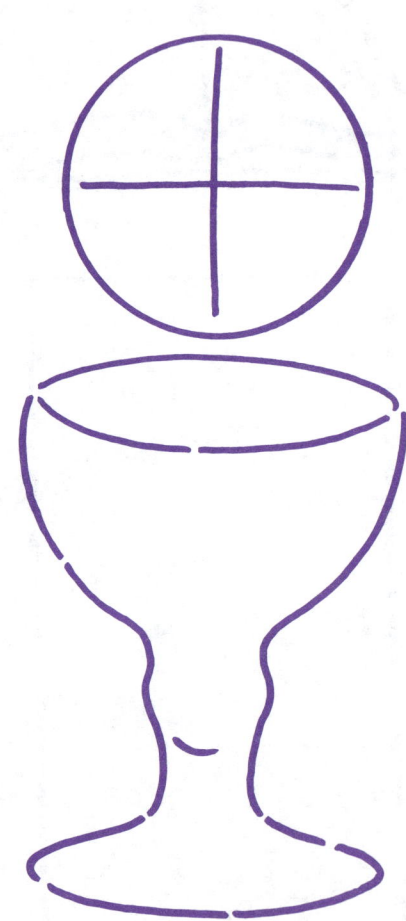

Eucharist, or Holy Communion, is not a one-time sacrament. We can celebrate this sacrament every day of our lives, if we want to! Just think how strong our gifts can be!

Write the names of the seven gifts of the Holy Spirit on these presents.

Isn't it great that God l _ _ _ _ us and
gives us g _ _ _ _ and wants us
to c _ _ _ _ _ _ _ _ _ with Him?

And if we choose to accept His gifts, grow in the Holy Spirit, and bear His fruit, then we will receive the greatest gift of all ...

... to live forever in heaven with God!

Parent-Teacher Guide

Understanding the Person of the Holy Spirit is difficult, even for many adults. Children can easily identify with God the Father because He is pictured as a father or grandfather. Since Jesus is God incarnate (which means He is truly God as well as truly human in all things but sin), children can easily picture Him, too. But the Holy Spirit has no simple analogy. The picture of a dove has been used, since that is a common image stemming from the reference in the Bible at the time of the baptism of Jesus. This book is an attempt to explain the role of the Holy Spirit in our lives, especially as it applies to the time of our confirmation. Specifically, it is aimed at very young children, and its goal is to give a general impression that can be developed more fully as a child grows. Receiving and opening gifts is a positive, concrete image that will help children grasp this important but difficult subject. This guide will give both the specific directions and answers for each page, as well as some background information and resources for the parent or teacher. Some children may want to color the illustrations as they discuss the subject matter with you, while for others this would be a distraction. Use your discretion.

For the benefit of parents and teachers who want to strengthen their own understanding of sacraments, and the role of the Holy Spirit, specific references to the *Catechism of the Catholic Church (CCC)* are included. Since the paragraphs in the *Catechism* are all numbered, it should be easy for anyone to look up these references. A copy of the *Catechism* should be available in the religious education department of your parish if you do not have one.

PAGE 1: The goal here is to have the child associate Confirmation with a positive memory of celebration. It can be a holiday like Christmas or a birthday, which usually involves gifts. Other simpler celebrations will work, too, because all celebrations have positive gifts, such as seeing special people or having special treats. Encourage the child to share what makes the occasion special.

PAGE 2: *Missing words*: <u>celebrate</u>, <u>presence</u>.

The love of God and His presence in our lives cannot be emphasized enough. It is the foundation upon which all the rest of Christian development is based. The acceptance that God not only "knows best" but also knows what will bring us true joy is what makes it easier to follow the Ten Commandments (*CCC* Part 3, Section 2, 2052-2557) and the corporal and spiritual works of mercy (*CCC* 2447).

PAGE 3: *The names of the sacraments are (the pictured clues are named)*: <u>Baptism</u> (water), <u>Confirmation</u> (dove), <u>Eucharist</u> (host and chalice), <u>Reconciliation</u> (handshake), <u>Holy Orders</u> (stole), <u>Anointing of the Sick</u> (person being anointed), and <u>Matrimony</u> (cross and rings).

If you would like to better understand any of the sacraments, how and when they are administered, and what their biblical base is, please refer to the *Catechism* (Part Two, Section Two, 1210-1690), which discusses sacraments of the Church. A Catholic definition of a sacrament can be found in a Catholic dictionary or the glossary of the second edition of the *Catechism*.

Please note that the word "Reconciliation" has been used for the sacrament called "Penance and Reconciliation" in the *Catechism*. This is to simplify the name and use the word that young children will most likely be familiar with. Please take a moment to make clear that the word "Penance" would also be correct.

PAGE 4: *Missing word*: <u>welcomed</u>.

Since the sacrament of Baptism should already have been discussed, the definition here is greatly simplified. The concept of cleansing from original sin, the imparting of grace, and becoming a part of the Mystical Body of Christ can be reviewed at this time by the parent or teacher, if so desired (*CCC* 1213-1216 — and further on, if needed).

PAGE 5: *Crossword answers*: 1. <u>Baptism</u>; 2. <u>welcomed</u>; 3. <u>Confirmation</u>; 4. <u>stronger</u>.

A complete adult explanation of the sacrament of Confirmation can be found in the *Catechism* (1285-1321).

PAGES 6 AND 7: The Church encourages us to administer sacraments to children as soon as they are able to be responsible for their choices (*CCC* 1307-1308).

Christian morality teaches that there are right and wrong choices. Contrary to "situation ethics," which allows people to do whatever feels right in a given situation, Christian morality requires us to form our conscience to reflect not what *we* feel is right, but what *Jesus* would see as right. This requires that we come to know God through prayer, sacraments, and study of Scripture and Holy Tradition. This is a lifelong process. At this time, encourage the child to think of situations that have a clear *right* choice, a choice that reflects knowledge of Jesus' character and what He would do. The choices may be as simple as sharing, or choosing to be kind rather than hurtful to others.

PAGE 8: *Missing word*: <u>celebration</u>.

PAGE 9: The story of Pentecost can be read from any Bible; if you have a children's Bible storybook that tells the story in simpler words and pictures, that may be even better. Help the child understand the transformation the apostles experienced, going from fearful men to confident ambassadors of Christ.

PAGES 10 AND 11: All of the words in the Wordfind have been used on these two pages, so this exercise is a review of the important concepts. The meanings behind the laying on of hands and anointing with chrism as well as being sealed with the Holy Spirit are explained in the *Catechism* (1287-1296).

A rite or tradition may have little meaning to children, unless we bring it to life for them. In discussing the history of the rites of Confirmation, most children respond to the idea that this is an unbroken tradition. Help them become excited about the fact that when the bishop anoints them, they are being touched by one who was touched by one who was touched ... all the way back to the ones who were "touched" or "anointed" by Christ and the Holy Spirit. In this unbroken way, the Spirit experienced at Pentecost continues to flow into us today.

PAGES 12-15: The names of the gifts of the Holy Spirit may seem like big words to some children. Every effort has been made to keep the definitions as simple as possible. The meanings of these gifts are very similar to one another. It might help to realize that each gift seems to build on the one before it, and sometimes to even overlap it. Take time to discuss these definitions with your children. One way to see if things make sense to them is to have the children try to explain something in their own words.

A good way to explain something is to use examples of when it is used in real life, which then can be written down on Pages 14 and 15. For example, piety calls us to put God first. For a child, this may mean saying a prayer of thanks before eating a treat or meal, or choosing to go to church without complaining so that he can pray and feel close to God.

For the gift of wisdom, one example could be when children don't get what they want. Rather than throwing a fit of complaining, they may try to see that God has something else in mind for them. They may have to be patient awhile before they know what it is.

Adults may want to prepare themselves in order to help their children. The dictionary definition of the words may differ from the one intended in the Bible. Here are some places in the Bible where these gifts are mentioned and discussed: **Isaiah 11:2-3a** (all gifts); **1 Timothy 6:11-16** (piety, fortitude); **Proverbs 8:13, 9:10, 14:26-27** (fear of the Lord, wisdom, knowledge, understanding, fortitude); **Colossians 1:9-12** (knowledge, wisdom, understanding, piety, fortitude); **1 Kings 3:4-14** (piety, understanding, wisdom); **Job 28:20-28** (wisdom, understanding, fear of the Lord); **Psalm 16:7-11** (counsel, piety, fortitude); **Psalm 18:2-4, 32-35** (fortitude).

A Catholic dictionary or the glossary in the second edition of the *Catechism* will also have definitions that may help.

PAGES 16-17: Discuss the importance of prayer. Name times that families pray, and times when individuals can or should pray. Remind the child that the Sign of the Cross is a prayer that restates our baptismal promises and reflects our belief in the three Persons of the Trinity. It is something simple that can be done anytime a person wants to feel closer to God. The entire fourth part of the *Catechism* is a discussion of Christian prayer, so it is a great source to answer any of your questions. This would be a great time to set some goals to pray more often.

PAGES 18-20: These fruits of the Holy Spirit are named in Galatians 5:22-23. (Earlier in Galatians, there is a description of the fruits of sin. It is up to the parent or teacher to decide if a discussion of the negative is appropriate at this time.) The children can color in the outlines around the words to make them look more like fruit. As they color, have the children try to explain what each word means, and help them with the ones they don't know. Then have them write the fruits in any order in the blanks on the following page. Make sure they understand that the analogy of "producing fruit" means living out, or doing, these good things in our lives (*CCC* 736).

PAGE 21: Have the children trace the letters of the prayer and then read it to you. You can have the children make up their own prayers to help them feel comfortable with the idea of spontaneous prayer to God. Some children may be ready to memorize the full prayer to the Holy Spirit found in Catholic prayer books.

PAGES 22-24: These pages try to simplify the Mass into recognizable parts. Discuss the Mass with your children, and help them remember the times during the Mass when we pray with and for one another; when we read from the Bible; and when the consecration occurs, as plain bread and wine are changed into the Body and Blood of Jesus. Use the missal booklets during Mass to show them the different parts, which may help them keep an interest in what is happening. Teach them how to follow along so that they can feel involved.

On Page 24, rays of light can be added to the picture of the host and chalice to emphasize the transformation that occurs during the Mass. Children can use brightly colored crayons, or things like gel pens or glitter if you have them.

PAGE 25: This is simply review. Have the children turn back to Page 13 if they need help remembering the names of the gifts of the Holy Spirit.

PAGE 26: *Missing words*: <u>loves</u>, <u>gifts</u>, <u>celebrate</u>.

Page 27: This may be a good time to check what the children think about heaven. If there have been loved ones who have died, this might be a good time to discuss that in heaven we will all be safe together forever. Be sure to ask the children if there are any questions about anything in the book. You don't have to know the answers. If any hard questions come up, simply admit that you aren't sure, and then look it up together, or promise to find the answer and talk about it later.

God bless you for taking the time to help others know more about our wonderful God!